Tithing
Giving
and
Prosperity

Dr. Roy B. Blizzard is president of Bible Scholars, Inc., an Austin-based corporation dedicated to biblical research and education. He is the author of *The Bible Sex and You, Mishnah and the Words of Jesus, The Mountain of the Lord, Let Judah go up first: A study in praise, prayer, and worship*, and coauthor of *Understanding the Difficult Words of Jesus: New Insights From a Hebrew Perspective*. Visit the Bible Scholars website at www.biblescholars.org.

Tithing
Giving
and
Prosperity

Roy B. Blizzard

Bible Scholars, Inc.
Austin, Texas

Cover design: Sue Schoenfeld

P.O. Box 204073
Austin, Texas 78720
www.biblescholars.org

CONTENTS

CHAPTER 1
PROSPERITY AND TITHING

P eople, by their very nature, are dreamers. They dream of greatness, success, fulfillment. Many of our dreams center around achievement of what are worthy and desirable goals. We dream of successful human relationships, marital bliss, the perfect family, recognition by peers, material possessions, or, in short, of prosperity.

But, what is prosperity? Unfortunately, there is a great deal of misunderstanding on this subject among God's people today. Many honest, sincere, and well-meaning people are teaching on prosperity and the related subjects of tithing and giving. Sadly, much of what is being taught is in error and is a distortion of the biblical perspective concerning these matters.

Prosperity! It's an important subject and one which is of interest to most normal individuals. I am interested in prosperity – for myself, and for my family. I personally, as I am sure many other parents have, have gone to great lengths and considerable sacrifice to ensure that my children and their children should be prosperous. And likewise, I believe that it is God's desire that all of His children prosper. I believe he has gone to great lengths and unparalleled sacrifices to ensure the prosperity of His children. The *Bible* tells us that the Lord has "pleasure in the prosperity of His servants" (*Psalm* 35:27). The Apostle John, in his third epistle, verse 2, reflects this Godly desire when he writes, "Beloved, I wish above all things that you may prosper."

God's desire that His children should prosper is further reflected in such passages as:

> Ask, and it shall be given you; seek, and you shall find; knock, and it shall be opened unto you: for everyone that asks receives, and he that seeks finds, and to him that knocks it shall be opened. Or, what man is there of you whom, if his son ask bread, will he give him a stone? Or if he ask fish, will he give him a serpent? If you then being evil, know how to give good gifts unto your children, how much more shall your Father which is in heaven give good things to them that ask Him? (*Matthew* 7:7-11).

> And all things, whatsoever you shall ask in prayer, believing, you shall receive (*Matthew* 21:22).

Judging from these and similar passages of Scripture, I think we can safely conclude that God desires that all of His people prosper. And, that is exactly what we are being told. Some of the "biggest names in the business" have made prosperity, tithing, or "seed faith giving" central themes in their teaching. I am sure that most of us have heard or read statements similar to the following:

> "If you have a need, go out and find someone who is

needy and give something away, for God is obligated to return unto you as you have given."

"Now, I know many of you out there have needs. If you expect to be able to pay your bills by the first of next month, you need to rush in your offerings so we can receive them by the tenth of this month."

"Send in your 'seed faith' offering, and when you do, remember, God is obligated to return unto you one hundredfold according to His word."

The latter statement is a veiled reference to *Matthew* 19:29 and its parallel passage in *Mark* 10:30.

The unfortunate result of such teaching is that people are arriving at two mistaken conclusions:

1. The more we give, the more we will receive back from God; and
2. The more spiritual we are, the more prosperous we are or will be.

Therefore, according to this logic, if a person has been blessed materially, accumulating a large number of possessions, that person must be spiritual. The more one has, the more spiritual he is. If one is able to fly around the country in an airplane, drive a new Cadillac, and live in a big house – in short, if one is prosperous – then that is an indication of spirituality .

This type of thinking brings with it corresponding problems. Many people begin to identify prosperity with the accumulation of material possessions. Such an erroneous conclusion places a tremendous spiritual burden on the child of God. They reason as follows: God intends for His children to prosper. I am not prospering as I am told I should, so there must be something wrong with me spiritually.

Even more potentially dangerous is that special individual for whom everything works. He is prospering, he is successful – in some instances wildly so – all of which he attributes to the special favor he has with God. He often begins to view himself as some "chosen" vessel of God. As his success is translated into theology, he begins to operate according to emotion and experience rather than on knowledge of the biblical text or sound business principles. Frequently, he winds up foolishly following a special spiritual "guru" or losing or giving away much of his fortune foolishly. Or, even worse, he winds up as a sought after speaker or *Bible* teacher.

Many evangelists and teachers are leaving these types of false impressions in the believers' minds. Of course, in most instances it is quite unintentional. The evangelists or teachers are honest and sincere in their beliefs; the problem arises in their ignorance of the correct biblical perspective on the subject. Regardless of their fame or popularity, most of the teaching promulgated today on the subject of prosperity and tithing is fundamentally in error.

I know personally many whose faith has been shaken because of this teaching. One typical case is that of a pastor who decided that he needed a new car. In "seed faith" he gave his old car away, believing that God was obligated to return unto him "one hundredfold." After several years of waiting and believing, he began to lose faith.

Another instance involved a young couple who needed new furniture. In "seed faith," they gave all their old furniture away, believing that God was obligated to return a "hundredfold," which, of course, they interpreted as a house full of new furniture. After several months of sitting on orange crates and sleeping on the floor, they began to doubt God and their faith. As a direct result of this experience, their marriage ultimately ended in divorce.

Closely related to this teaching on prosperity is the subject of tithing. The child of God has been spiritually browbeaten with this subject for centuries. We have been told that if we are really spiritual – if we really want to prosper – then the place to begin is with the tithe. That is the one-tenth that we 'owe' God. We must make sure that the first one-tenth is taken out before anything else, and that it goes directly into the "storehouse" (i.e., the church we are attending, or the ministry to which we are listening). Then, if we are truly spiritual, we will do more than tithe; we will also give offerings. Offerings, in most instances, can be dispensed according to personal judgment – but the tithe must be given to the church!

The time has come for this subject to be correctly treated and placed in its proper perspective. And frankly, it is not all that difficult to do. All that we have to do is look at the subject in its historical and biblical context. We must view prosperity and tithing through the eyes of Judaism.

I believe that the best place to begin is with the subject of tithing, and then move in logical progression to giving, and finally, prosperity.

CHAPTER 2
TITHING AND GIVING

The word "tithe" is the Hebrew word *ma'aser*, which means "the tenth", and refers to the giving of one-tenth of one's produce or possessions. The tithe was a tax imposed by temple authorities and collected by official temple representatives. It was usually stored in the temple treasury or storehouse, over which temple functionaries were in charge. Generally speaking, the food stores, grain, agricultural products, and so forth, were utilized by the priest and other temple personnel. Animals tithed to the temple were largely used in ritual sacrifice.

Tithing is not something new or exclusive to the *Bible*. The concept of the tithe is well documented in non-biblical literature from the ancient Middle East. The receiving of the tithe as sacred "temple tax" is documented in both neo-Babylonian (c. 6th century BCE) and in Syro-Palestine documents (c. 14th century BCE). It is also seen in written records from Ugarit as a "royal" tax, imposed by the king and used for upkeep of the court. It is a blending of these two traditions, i.e., the "sacred" tax on the one hand, and the "royal" tax on the other that develops in the *Bible* among the Hebrew people, the nation of Israel, and in later Judaism.

DEVELOPMENT OF THE BIBLICAL CONCEPT OF TITHING

TITHING IN THE PATRIARCHAL AGE

The first mention of tithing in the *Bible* is in *Genesis* 14, which recounts the meeting of Abraham and Melchizedek, the priest-king of the city of Salem (ancient Jerusalem). It is important to understand exactly who Melchizedek was. First, he was not an angelic or supernatural being, and second, he was not an incarnation of Christ. He was simply the priest-king of Salem, and a worshipper of El Elyon, the most high God, or *YHWH*. His name in Hebrew, *Malchi Tzedek*, means "my king is righteous," and it is undoubtedly a reference to his relationship with El Elyon. In Melchizedek we see the blending of the two ancient traditions relative to the tithe, namely, the "sacred" and the "royal."

Why did Abraham pay tithes to Melchizedek of all he had? Who told Abraham to do this? Because the collection of the temple tax or royal tax was a common practice in Abraham's day, one might assume that it was just "understood" that such would be required of him, given the place and person of Melchizedek. However, I believe the real answer is much more significant, and that it establishes the principle of tithing that runs through the biblical text.

The fact is, no one told Abraham to pay tithes to Melchizedek. Abraham gave the tithe to Melchizedek because he wanted to. This is demonstrated in the following passage:

And Melchizedek king of Salem brought forth bread and wine: and he was the priest of the most high God. And he blessed him and said, Blessed be Abram of the most high God, possessor of heaven and earth: And blessed be the most high God, which hath delivered thine enemies into thy hand. And he [Abram] gave him tithes of all (*Genesis* 14:18-20).

Abraham gave because he had been blessed and wanted to be a blessing in return! Abraham's giving was strictly voluntary, with no motive of receiving anything in return.

An interesting and important point regarding Abraham's tithe to Melchizedek is noted by Selden in his excellent work, *The Historie of Tithes*, published in 1618. He notes that the phrase in the Hebrew text, "and gave him a tithe of all" (*Genesis* 14:20), refers only to the spoils he had taken in rescuing his nephew, Lot (Selden 1618: 1, 2). This is also repeated by Josephus:

And when Abram gave the tenth part of his prey, he accepted of the gift (Josephus, Ant. 1, X, 2).

The next instance of tithing is in *Genesis* 28:22, when Jacob vows: "...and of all that thou shalt give me, I will surely give the tenth unto thee." Who told Jacob he was obliged to return the tenth or pay the tithe? Further, to whom did Jacob vow to pay the tithe? How was it to be paid? How was it to be collected? And by whom was it to be utilized? Again, Selden notes:

Into whose he gave his Tithes, appears not, but the chiefest Priest of that time was his father, Isaac. For before Aaron, the Jews say, the Priesthood was wholly annext to the first born of families (Selden 1618: 5).

15

In the early stages of the development of the biblical concept of tithing, we see in the first instance, with Abraham, that the tithe is given of Abraham's own free will. In Jacob's case, the tithe is clearly linked with a vow or, again, a voluntary gift. It is only much later and under much different circumstances that the tithe begins to take the form of an obligatory gift or tax.

TITHING IN THE MOSAIC LAW

From the time of the Mosaic Law, the subject of tithing becomes increasingly complex. In *Leviticus* 27:30-34, we find what is perhaps the earliest of the Mosaical laws relating to the tithe:

> And all the tithe of the land, whether of the seed of the land, or of the fruit of the tree, is the Lord's: it is holy unto the Lord. And if a man will at all redeem aught of his tithes, he shall add thereto the fifth part thereof.
>
> And concerning the tithe of the herd, or of the flock, even whatsoever passeth under the rod, the tenth shall be holy unto the Lord. He shall not search whether it be good or bad, neither shall he change it: and if he change it at all, then both it and the change shall be holy; it shall not be redeemed. These are the commandments, which the Lord commanded Moses for the children of Israel in Mount Sinai.

Under the Levitical code, the tithe becomes the property of the Lord and is offered as a gift to Him. However, in *Leviticus* 23:20, *Numbers* 5:8, and numerous other passages in both *Leviticus* and *Numbers*, it may be safely stated that "gifts to the Lord" and "gifts to priests" are synonymous:

But if the man hath no kinsman to recompense the trespass unto, let the trespass be recompensed unto the LORD, even to the priest... (*Numbers* 5:8).

Accordingly, the tithe is considered to be the property of the Sanctuary and the priesthood that ministers to it.

With the entrance of the Israelites into the land, it seems the concept of the tithe is expanded to include all Levites, even those who were not officiating at the Sanctuary.

And, behold, I have given the children of Levi all the tenth in Israel for an inheritance, for their service which they serve, even the service of the tabernacle of the congregation. Neither must the children of Israel henceforth come nigh the tabernacle of the congregation, lest they bear sin, and die.

But the Levites shall do the service of the tabernacle of the congregation, and they shall bear their iniquity: it shall be a statute for ever throughout your generations, that among the children of Israel they shall have no inheritance.

But the tithes of the children of Israel, which they offer as a heave offering unto the Lord, I have given to the Levites to inherit: therefore I have said unto them: Among the children of Israel they shall have no inheritance (*Numbers* 18:21-23).

This inclusion of all Levites was undoubtedly due, as reflected in the passage above, to the fact that they had no specific inheritance in the Promised Land. As is seen in *Joshua* 21, certain cities were designated as "Levitical Cities." During this period, and on into the United Hebrew Monarchy with David and Solomon, these cities probably served as "royal" cities where Temple warehouses and granaries were overseen by the Levites. As such, we see a blending of the "royal" and the "sacred" tax in support of both the Holy Sanctuary and of the Levites who supervised the distribution of the tithes.

The regulations governing the tithe, as recorded in *Deuteronomy* 14:22-29, are quite different from those in *Numbers*. It is possible that the regulations in *Deuteronomy* reflect the situation in Israel after the United Monarchy, during which time the Levitical cities and the religious centers were abandoned, making the tithe no longer necessary to their maintenance. For the present at least, we will view the matter in the historical development of the nation of Israel, and later look at how the Rabbis dealt with this apparent contradiction between the regulations in *Numbers* 18 and *Deuteronomy* 14.

Thou shall truly tithe all the increase of thy seed, that the field bringeth forth year by year.

And thou shall eat before the Lord thy God, in the place which he shall choose to place his name there, the tithe of thy corn, of thy wine, and of thine oil, and the firstlings of thy herds and of thy flocks; that thou mayest learn to fear the Lord thy God always.

And if the way be too long for thee, so thou are not able to carry it; or if the place be too far from thee, which the Lord thy God shall choose to set his name there, when the Lord thy God hath blessed thee:

Then shall thou turn it into money, and bind up the money in thy hand, and shalt go unto the place which the Lord thy God shall choose:

And thou shalt bestow that money for whatsoever thy soul lusteth after, for oxen, or for sheep, or for wine, or for strong drink, or for whatsoever thy soul desireth: and thou shall eat there before the Lord thy God, and thou shall rejoice, thou, and thine household,

And the Levite that is within thy gates; thou shall not forsake him; for he hath no part nor inheritance with thee.

At the end of three years thou shalt bring forth all the tithe of thine increase the same year, and shalt lay it up within thy gates:

And the Levites, (because he hath no part nor inheritance with thee,) and the stranger, and fatherless, and the widow, which are within thy gates, shall come, and shall eat and be satisfied; that the Lord thy God may bless thee in all the work of thine hand which thou doest (*Deuteronomy* 14:22-29).

Note in the Deuteronomic injunction that the tithe was on the increase of the field only. This tithe was to be taken by the landowner and his family and eaten before the Lord in the city of the Sanctuary, i.e., Temple. However, if the distance was too great to practically transport the tithe, it could be converted to money and spent on "whatsoever thy soul desireth," as long as it was eaten before the Lord with thanksgiving. Note, however, a very important difference: every third year the tithes were to be kept home to feed the "Levite, the stranger, and the fatherless, and the widow." In other words, the tithe of every third year was to be kept at home to minister to the needs of the poor and needy as well as the Levite. Since the seventh year was the Sabbath year and no tithing was permitted, the tithe of the first, second, fourth and fifth years was eaten before the Lord at the Sanctuary by the landowner, but the tithe of the third and sixth years was stored at home for the poor and needy.

I think it is proper to note here a point in our study so important that it cannot be overemphasized. There is a principle being set forth here that will pervade the whole of historical Judaism and supersede the rules and regulations of tithing itself, and that is the concept of "*tzedakah*," or "charity" – the concept in Judaism of the responsibility of the individual to give to the needs of others. This important concept will be stressed as we progress further in our study.

During the period of the Divided Kingdom (circa 931 BC-586 BC), the Israelites often transferred tithes due to God to pagan deities as is indicated in *Amos* 4:4ff. However, in the Southern Kingdom of Judah, a righteous king might impose the tithe on the people, either to strengthen the kingdom or in the way of religious revival. Such can be seen from *2 Chronicles* 31:6-12, during the reform of Hezekiah.

After the period of the exile and the return, the call again goes out to the people to bring "all the tithes into the storehouse" (*Malachi* 3:10). During the time of the rebuilding of the city and the walls in the days of Ezra and Nehemiah, the tithe and its collection (again as a sacred tax) were necessary to strengthen the national and economic status of the city of Jerusalem (see *Nehemiah* 13:4-13). From *Nehemiah* 10:38 we see how the Levites were enlisted as tax collectors to receive the tithes and bring them to the main Sanctuary at Jerusalem. In *Nehemiah* 13:13 we also learn that Nehemiah placed the Levites in charge of the distribution of the tithes.

TITHING DURING THE SECOND TEMPLE PERIOD

As we move in our study into the Second Temple Period (from the rebuilding of the Temple in 516 BCE until its destruction in 70 CE) and on into the Rabbinic period, we will note in the historical development of the tithe a move from sacralization, or the sacred, to secularization, with all the rules and regulations of Rabbinic law.

According to the Rabbis, all the books of Moses, including both *Numbers* and *Deuteronomy*, were the "law given to Moses at Sinai" (*Avot* 1:1). Therefore, there could be no basic conflict between the two. So, the Rabbis combined the material from both *Numbers* and *Deuteronomy*. According to Rabbinic Law, or *halachah*, there were two basic kinds of offerings: the "*terumah*", or the "heave offering" and the "tithe." Before any produce of the ground was considered fit for consumption, both the *terumah* and the tithe had to be duly offered.

According to the Rabbis, the *terumah* had to be set aside for priests. There was no specific injunction on what constituted a proper *terumah*, so the Rabbis determined:

The proper amount of the *terumah*:

If a man is liberal [literally, "good eye"], it is one-fortieth. But Shammai says one-thirtieth: for the average man it is one-fiftieth, and for the miserly [literally, "evil eye"], one-sixtieth (*Terumah* 4:3).*

Although in *Deuteronomy* 12:17 the *terumah* and tithe (*ma'aser*) applied only to grain, wine, and oil, the Rabbis concluded that it also applied to other produce and fruits as well as vegetables.

Whatever is food and does not grow wild and grows from the earth is liable to tithes (*Ma'aser* 1:1).

At the end of the 2nd century CE, the tithe was extended to money as well.

*For a treatment of the Hebrew idioms "good eye" and "bad eye," see David Bivin and Roy Blizzard Jr., *Understanding the Difficult Words of Jesus: New Insights From a Hebrew Perspective*, Destiny Image Publishers, 2001, 144-145.

After the *terumah*, or heave offering, had been set aside, a tenth was taken from what was left and was given to the Levites as stated in *Numbers* 18:21ff. This tithe was designated as the "first tithe," or *ma'aser rishon*. The Levites then had to give a tithe of this "first tithe" to the priests, which was called "a tithe of the tithes." From what remained of the original amount, a "second tithe" (*ma'aser sheni*) was taken, which was to be taken up to Jerusalem and eaten there or redeemed for money and spent in Jerusalem. This was to be done in the first, second, fourth, and fifth years of the seven-year cycle. In the third and sixth years, the "tithe for the poor" (*ma'aser ani*) was kept at home for the poor and needy. Accordingly, in addition to the *terumah*, two tithes were taken each year, except in the seventh year when no tithes were received. Although no specific time was designated for the receiving of the tithes, it can be assumed that they were taken to Jerusalem during the three pilgrim festivals, i.e., Passover, Pentecost, and Tabernacles.

An example of how this worked is illustrated by Selden as follows:

After the first fruits paid in years, admit:

The increase 6,000. Ephaphs: the heave offering [*terumah*] at least must be 100.

The remainder 5,900. The First Tithe, 590, and out of this, 59 to the Priests.

The remainder 5,310. Out of this, the Second Tithe. 531 which every two years the Levites had at Jerusalem, and every third year was spent in the gates of the husbandmen.

So that of 6,000 Ephaphs, the Levites and poor had in all 1,062 whole to themselves, the Priests, 159, and the husbandmen only 4,779. He yearly thus paid more than a sixth part of his increase, beside first-fruits; almost a fifth. Many of no small name, grossly slip in reckoning and dividing these kinds of their Tithe. But this here delivered, is from the holy text and the Jewish Lawyers (Selden 1618:17).

Although a great deal of importance was placed on the offering of the *terumah* and the *ma'aser* by the religious leaders, it seems clear that during the latter part of the 2nd and 1st centuries BCE, the people had already grown lax in the giving of the tithe. According to a personal interview the author had in Jerusalem with Professor Shmuel Safrai, noted author and Jewish historian of the Second Temple Period, the people had already started paying the tithes to their own local priest, rabbis, and scholars, whether the latter two were Levites or not. The idea, of course, was to support those who were in charge of spiritual leadership.

It is important to note that according to *halachah*, the duty of setting aside *terumah* and *ma'aser* did not apply outside the land of Israel...which means that according to Jewish law, the laws and regulations concerning tithing applied only to Eretz Israel, or the land of Israel. The reason being:

Every precept dependent on the land of Israel is in force both within and without the land of Israel except for *orlah* [the fruit of a tree of the first three years] and *kilayim* [forbidden junctions] (*Kiddushin* 1:9).

In practice, however, the tithe was observed in Syria, Babylon, Egypt, and the lands of Moab and Ammon.

After the destruction of the Temple, the tithe continued to be set aside as a kind of substitute for the Temple sacrifice. However, the tithe began to be used more and more not just for the priests and Levites, but to support the local spiritual leaders such as rabbis and scholars, and to minister to the poor and needy in the local community. Thus, we see the concept of the tithe merging and blending more and more into the whole concept of *tzedakah*, or charity, previously mentioned. This idea develops to such a degree that by the 18th century some have concluded:

> Tithing one's earnings is simply a custom and is not obligatory either under the Mosaic or under the rabbinical law. The whole of the tithe must be given to the poor; and no part of it may be appropriated to any other religious purpose (*The Jewish Encyclopedia*, vol. XII, 152).

> After the second Temple was destroyed, and the dispersion of the Jews, their Law of first fruits, *terumahs*, and tithes, with them ceased...

> ...Rabbi Ben Maimon [ca. 1135-1204] stated, 'At this day by their law they pay none; Those that live in their land of Israel, for want of their Priesthood and Temple; those that live dispersed other countries, both for that reason, as also for the other which restrain the payment of them to Canaan, and herein all agree' (Selden 1618:21).

TITHING IN THE EARLY CHURCH

Whatever else may be said about the institution of tithing, one important fact cannot be overemphasized. It was strictly a religious institution within the framework of historic Judaism, and was never adopted by the early 1st century Church as a means of funding the operation of the fellowship of the saints nor the support of the functionaries of the Church.

In the Gospels, any references that are made to tithing are done so in a strictly Jewish context. After the establishment of the Church on the day of Pentecost, the subject of tithing is never mentioned in the context of the practice of the early Church. In *Acts* 2:42,45 we can see the precedent established that the early Church will follow:

> And they continued steadfastly in the Apostle's doctrine and fellowship, and in breaking of bread, and in prayers...And [they] sold their possessions and parted them to all men, as every man had need.

Two points are of interest and importance. One, the usage of the term "fellowship" (*koinonia*) and, secondly, that goods were distributed according to need. The Greek word used in *Acts* 2:42, *koinonia*, is used elsewhere in the *New Testament* for "contribution":

The concept of tithing as a means of the support of the Church or church functionaries is a much later development, as we shall note later.

> For it hath pleased them of Macedonia and Achaia to make a certain contribution (*koinonia*) for the poor saints which are at Jerusalem (*Romans* 15:26).

We see the practice of *Acts* 2:42 echoed and amplified in the writings of Justin Martyr. Justin Martyr was born about 110 CE, shortly after the end of the Apostolic Age, and lived until 165 CE. He was born in Samaria, the ancient capital of the Northern Kingdom of Israel. Martyr was a true genius, a fervent Christian, and a prolific writer and apologist. With him, we mark the beginning of the "sub-apostolic age." In his "First Apology," he records the activity of the early believers in the land of Israel. Note in the following quote from "First Apology" two things: first, the similarity to *Acts* 2:42, and second, the Jewish nature of their assembly.

> And on the day called Sunday, all who live in cities or in the country gather together to one place, and the memoirs of the apostles or the writings of the prophets are read [apostle's doctrine], as long as time permits; then, when the reader has ceased, the president [nasi, or president of the synagogue] verbally instructs, and exhorts to the imitation of these good things. Then we all rise together and pray [prayers], and, as we have before said, when our prayer is ended, bread and wine and water are brought, and the president in like manner offers prayers and thanksgivings, according to his ability, and the people assent, saying Amen; and there is a distribution to each, and a participation of that over which thanks have been given [Lord's Supper, or the "breaking of bread"], and to those who are absent a portion is sent by the deacons. And they who are well to do, and willing, give what each thinks fit; and what is collected is deposited with the president, who succors the orphans and widows, and those who, through sickness or any other cause, are in want, and those who are in

bonds, and the strangers sojourning among us, and in a word takes care of all who are in need [collection/contribution = *koinonia*]" (*The Ante-Nicene Fathers*, vol. I, Eerdmans, 186).

This concept of "free will offerings" as an act of *tzedakah* or righteousness – the responsibility of believer to believer – is echoed in other writings of *The Ante-Nicene Fathers* and in some instances, as we will note, indicate the acceptance or the non-acceptance of the believer by Almighty God. On at least one occasion, *Matthew* 25:34 is extensively quoted to emphasize the responsibility of the believer to minister to the needs of others, and further, that this willingness and ministry is a prerequisite to hearing that "Come ye blessed of my Father, inherit the kingdom prepared for you from the foundations of the world" (*The Ante-Nicene Fathers*, vol. V, Eerdmans, 437). From the "Constitution of the Holy Apostles" (second half of the 3rd century), this concept is echoed in the following passages:

> But if ye say that those who give alms are such as these, and if we do not receive from them, whence shall we administer to the widows? And whence shall the poor among the people be maintained? But if a gift be wanting, inform the brethren, and make a collection from them, and thence minister to the orphans and widows in righteousness (*tzedakah*) (*The Ante-Nicene Fathers*, vol. VII, Eerdmans, 435).

And again:

> All the first fruits (*terumah*) of the wine-press, the threshing-floor, the oxen, and the sheep, shalt thou give to the priests, that thy storehouses and garners

and the products of thy land may be blessed, and thou mayest be strengthened with corn and wine and oil, and the herds of thy cattle and flocks of thy sheep may be increased. Thou shalt give the tenth [*ma'aser*] of thy increase to the orphan, and to the widow, and to the poor, and to the stranger. All the first-fruits [*terumah*] of thy hot bread, of thy barrels of wine, or oil, or honey, or nuts, or grapes, or the first-fruits of other things, shalt thou give to the priests; but those of silver, and of garments, and of all sort of possessions, to the orphans and to the widows (*The Ante-Nicene Fathers*, vol. VII, Eerdmans, 471).

Note again that the funds and/or goods collected went principally to minister to the needs of the saints, and not to the maintenance of an ecclesiastical system.

Another interesting and pertinent statement is found in Book II, sec. V, of the *Constitution of the Holy Apostles*, in which the writer quotes from *Matthew* 5:20:

"Unless your righteousness abound more than that of the scribes and the Pharisees, ye shall by no means enter into the Kingdom of heaven." Now herein will your righteousness exceed theirs, if you take greater care of the priests, orphans, and the widows; as it is written: "He hath scattered abroad; he hath given to the poor; his righteousness remaineth forever." And again: by acts of righteousness [*tzedakah*] and faith iniquities are purged." And again: Every bountiful soul is blessed. So therefore shalt thou do as the Lord has appointed, and shalt give to the priest what things are due to him, the first-fruits of thy floor, and of thy wine-press, and sin offerings, as to the mediator between God and such as stand in need of purgation and forgiveness. For it is thy duty to give, and his to administer, and being the administrator and disposer of ecclesiastical affairs (*The Ante-Nicene Fathers*, vol. VII, Eerdmans, 413).

From these statements from the 2nd and 3rd centuries, CE, we can see how the early Christians saw a relationship between the pattern of giving under the Law and their responsibilities in giving under Grace. The references to the first-fruits is, of course, a reference to the *terumah*, or "heave offering" of the Law. That they were aware of their responsibility to provide for the needs of the spiritual leaders is also quite clear. What is more important, however, for the Body of Believers today is the concept the early Church had of *koinonia* (Greek), or *tzedakah* (Hebrew), in ministering to the needs of others.

Koinonia belongs to the *koinos* group of Greek words. The main element is that of fellowship. The word is especially adopted to express an inner relationship. *Koinonia* denotes a participation, a close bond. It expresses a two-sided relationship with the emphasis either on the giving or on the receiving. It means either a participation or an impartation. Therefore, according to the Apostle Paul (*Romans* 12:13; 15:27; *1 Corinthians* 16:1,2), fellowship with Jesus implies a mutual fellowship with every other member of the family of God. In Jesus there is a close bond, a union that implies not only a spiritual union in the faith, but a further obligation to join in a living participation in the needs of the saints, whoever and wherever they might be. Hence Paul uses this term, *koinonia*, for collection. It is not just a financial matter, but is at the very depth of the spiritual meaning of fellowship. That fellowship, true *koinonia*, is expressed by the believer in both participation and impartation, freely and unequivocally offered.

The testimony of the practice of the Jews in the latter part of the Second Temple Period (3rd - 2nd centuries BCE) as well as that of the Apostle Paul, the early Church in the Land of Israel, and the writings of the *Ante-Nicene Fathers* all witness to the voluntary nature of giving. Again, not as matter of imposed "LAW," but as a responsibility in *tzedakah*. The true child of God recognized a responsibility that went beyond and superseded "Law" to minister to the needs of others. And further, there was that sense – that knowing – that as they blessed others, so too, would they be blessed.

It was, in fact, this very attitude of the early believer that accounted for the rapid spread of Christianity in the 1st century. In a world filled with unrest and hatred, the early believers practiced charity (*tzedakah*), hospitality, and brotherly love. In a world divided basically into two separate classes, the rich and the poor, the slave and the master, the equality of all men before God was of special appeal to the ignored and unloved masses.

So liberal, in the beginning of Christianity, was the devotion of the believers, that their bounty, to the evangelical priesthood, far exceeded what the tenth could have been. For if you look at the first of the Apostolic times; then the unity of heart among them, about Jerusalem, was such that all was common and none wanted, and "as many as were possessors of lands or houses, sold them and brought the price of the things that were sold and laid it down at the Apostles feet, and it was distributed unto every man according as he had need" [*Acts* 4:34] (Selden 1618:36).

Selden continues:

So in Galatia and in Corinth, where St. Paul ordained that weekly offerings for the Saints should be given by every man as he had thrived in his estate [*1 Cor.* 16:2]. By example of these, the course of monthly offerings succeeded in the next ages. Those Monthly Offerings given by devout and able Christians, the Bishops or Officers appointed in the Church, received; and carefully and charitably disposed them on Christian worship, the maintenance of the Clergy, feeding, clothing, and burying their poor brethren, widows, orphans, persons tyrannically condemned to the Mines, to Prisons, or banished by deportation to Isles (Selden 1618: 36,37).

Selden's last few words in this quote are interesting. Could it be it was in this manner that the Apostle John received his necessary sustenance while banished to the Isle of Patmos?

Selden continues to emphasize that these offerings called "stipes" (a word also used by the pagans in their temple offering) were voluntarily given, and then cites from the writings of Tertullian to lend additional support to the fact that in this early period, the offerings were both voluntary and freely given. But more importantly, they were used in support of the brethren in need and not of an ecclesiastical system, nor for the building of meeting houses.

Tertullian was born about 145 CE and became a Christian in 185 CE. He became a presbyter about 190 CE, and lived to a very old age, perhaps until 220 to 240 CE. Educated in Rome, he was one of the most notable of the church leaders of his day. He has often been referred to as the "founder of Latin Christianity." It was upon the foundations of the labors of Tertullian that Cyprian and, even later, Augustine built. In Tertullian's "Apology," he writes:

The tried men of our elders preside over us, obtaining that honor not by purchase, but by established character. There is no buying and selling of any sort in the things of God. Though we have our treasure-chest, it is not made up of purchase-money, as of a religion that has its price. On the monthly day [Sunday], if he likes, each puts in a small donation; but only if it be his pleasure, and only if he is able: for there is no compulsion; all is voluntary. These gifts are, as it were, piety's deposit fund. For they are not taken thence and spent on feasts, and drinking bouts, and eating-houses, but to support and bury poor people, to supply the wants of boys and girls destitute of means and parents, and of old persons confined now to the house; such too, as have suffered shipwreck; and if there happen to be any in the mines, or banished to the islands, or shut up in the prisons, for nothing but their fidelity to the cause of God's Church, they become the nurslings of their confession. But it is mainly the deeds of a love so noble that lead many to put a brand upon us. "See," they say, "how they love one another..." (*Ante-Nicene Fathers*, vol. III, Eerdmans, 46).

Again, note that in reading this statement of Tertullian, two familiar words come again to mind – voluntary and *tzedakah*.

TITHING FROM THE MIDDLE AGES ONWARD

We might ask then, how did the practice of the "Law of the tithe" creep into the structure of the organized Church and become, in most "Christian Churches," almost an ordinance akin to Baptism and the Lord's Supper?

As early as the second half of the 3rd century, ecclesiastical writers began to refer to the tithe of the *Old Testament* as a pattern, or example, for the Church to follow in support of the religious functionaries. Typical of these is the statement found in the *65ᵗʰ Epistle* of Cyprian.

Thascius Cyprian was born around 200 CE, converted in 246 CE, and assumed the office of Bishop of Carthage in 248 CE, which position he held until his martyrdom in 258 CE. In addressing a specific issue relative to the disposition of the last will and testament of a member of the clergy, he declares that clerics ought not to mingle in secular affairs, but follow the example of the Levitical priesthood:

> ...how much rather ought those not to be bound by worldly anxieties and involvements, who, being busied with divine and spiritual things, are not able to withdraw from the Church, and to have leisure for earthly and secular doings! The form of which ordination and engagement the Levites formerly observed under the law, so that when the eleven tribes divided the land and shared the possessions, the Levitical tribe, which was left free for the temple and the altar, and for the divine ministries, received nothing from that portion of the division; but while others cultivated the soil, that portion [the Levites] only cultivated the favor of God, and received the tithes from the eleven tribes, for their food and maintenance, from the fruits which grew. All which was done by divine authority and arrangement, so that they who waited on divine services might in no respect be called away, nor be compelled to consider or to transact secular business. Which plan and rule is now maintained in respect of the clergy, that they who are promoted by clerical ordination in the Church of the Lord may be called off in no respect from the divine administration, nor be tied down

by worldly anxieties and matters; but in the honor of the brethren who contribute, receiving, as it were, tenths of the fruits, they may not withdraw from the altars and sacrifices, but may serve day and night in heavenly and spiritual things (*Ante-Nicene Fathers*, vol. V, Eerdmans, 367).

Selden, who also quotes from this passage of Cyprian, correctly notes:

...that no payment of Tithes was in Cyprian's time in use, although some, too rashly, from this very place would infer too much (Selden 1618: 39).

From the evidence of the Scripture and the writings of the Apostles, had the Tithe been an ordinance or used by "the Church in Primitive times, Origin, Tertullian, and Cyprian (having such occasion to mention it) could not have been silent of it" (Selden 1618: 43).

The Earl of Selborne, in his book, *Ancient Facts And Fictions Concerning Churches and Tithes* (1892: 23,24), begins with these important statements:

Not tithes in particular, but all Church property, of every kind, was from early times, and down to the 14th century, described as "the patrimony [inherited estate] of the poor." The poor were always, and always must be, in an especial degree, objects of Christian ministry. To them "the Gospel" was to be "preached"...The relief, however, of the temporal as well as the spiritual wants of the destitute and the sick, the aged and afflicted, of strangers and foreigners, of prisoners and captives, was also, from the beginning, part of the office and work of the Church...Of tithes, there is no mention in the Western Church until the beginning of the 5th century; none, indeed, in this particular connection, until much later.

The Earl, whose name was Roundell Palmer, continues to give a detailed history of the development of tithes, drawing upon and adding to the earlier work of Selden.

According to Selden, the earliest example of a legal recognition of tithes in England was a decree of a synod in 786 (Selden 1618: 198ff).

In Henry Hallam's classic work, *View of the State of Europe During the Middle Ages* (1854), Hallam notes:

The slow and gradual manner in which parochial churches became independent, appears to be of itself a sufficient answer to those who ascribe a great antiquity to the universal payment of tithes. There are, however, more direct proofs that this species of ecclesiastical property was acquired not only by degrees, but with considerable opposition. We find the payment of tithes first enjoined by the canons of a provincial council in France near the end of the 6th century. From the 9th to the 12th, or even later, it is continually enforced by similar authority. Father Paul remarks, that most sermons preached about the 8th century inculcate this as a duty, and even seem to place the summit of Christian perfection in its performance. This reluctant submission of the people to a general and permanent tribute is perfectly consistent with the eagerness displayed by them in accumulating voluntary donations upon the church. Charlemagne was the first who gave the confirmation of a civil statute to these ecclesiastical injunctions; no one at least has, so far as I know, adduced any earlier law for the payment of tithes than one of his capitularies (Hallam 1854: 263,164).

This capitulary is known as *Baluzii Capitularia*, and dates from 789.

Charlemagne (742-814 CE), who was known in Latin as *Carolus Magnus* ("Charles the Great"), was king of the Franks from 768 to 814 and "Emperor of the Romans" from 800 to 814. He was one of the key figures in Medieval history. On Christmas day in 800, he was crowned Emperor of the Roman Empire by Pope Leo III. This act revived the concept of "empire" in the West, and the empire he revived lasted, in one form or another, for a thousand years. He was fiercely loyal to the Roman Catholic Church and far more powerful than the successors of Constantine had been. His capitulary regulated the tithe and divided it into three parts: one for the bishop and his clergy, the second for the poor, and the third for the support of the fabric of the Church.

In the course of time, the principle of payment of tithes was extended far beyond its original intention. It became very common to appropriate tithes, which had originally been payable to the bishop, either towards the support of particular churches, or, according to prevalent superstition, to monastic foundations (Hallam 1854:264).

Thus, they became transferable to laymen and saleable like ordinary property, in spite of the injunctions of the third Lateran Council [1179], and they became payable out of sources of income which were not originally tithable (*The Encyclopedia Britannica*, Eleventh Edition, 1911: 1,020).

The payment of tithes had been originally confined to those called "predial," or the fruits of the earth, but now was extended to every species of profit and to the wages of every kind of labor (Hallam 1854:264).

In the years following the third Lateran Council various discussions arose over what was tithable and what was not, who was exempt from payment, sale of rights to exact tithes from laymen, etc., until the time of Boniface VIII (1294-1303). Under Boniface, radical changes were made after he ascended to the papal chair. In the Unam Sanctam Bull of November 1302, Boniface made papal claim to world supremacy. He declared that if the king resists the pope, he resists God Himself. The following sentence of Thomas Aquinas was incorporated in the bull: "We declare define, and affirm that every man must obey the pope or forfeit his salvation." A synod held at Rome declared this bull to give a correct expression of the view of the Roman Catholic Church (Qualben 1960: 189). In addition, many questions that had arisen over the subject of tithes were settled by Boniface VIII.

By the time of Boniface VIII, the pope had vast financial resources at his command in addition to simony and the sale of indulgences. Indulgences were sold for the purpose of lightening, or remitting altogether, punishment in Purgatory for the sins of the living and those already in Purgatory. The practice of the sale of indulgences rested on the doctrine that Christ and his Saints had performed more good works than were needed. These surplus deeds of righteousness were at the disposal of the Church and could be sold to less fortunate or less righteous people.

Some of the additional resources available to the pope were:

1. The Annates, or first fruits, the first year's income in office, exacted of bishops and abbots;
2. The Reservations, the richest benefices in each country, were reserved for the use of the pope and the cardinals;
3. The Expectancies, in which the pope sold to the highest

bidder the nomination as successor to rich benefices before the death of the incumbent;

4. The Commendations, consisting of indefinite, provisional appointments on condition of payment of an annual tax;

5. The Jus spoliorum, or the claim that the pope was the rightful heir to all property acquired by officials of the Church during their tenure in office.

6. Tithing of church property for urgent wants (Qualben 1960: 188,189).

Individual priests now exacted tithes of all the income of the peasants and also demanded payment for such services as baptism, marriage, confession, extreme unction, and burial. Even the forgiveness of sins could be bought for money, in direct opposition to the teaching of the *New Testament* that a man is not redeemed with silver and gold, but with the precious blood of the Lord Jesus (*1 Peter* 1: 18,19). The Council of Trent (1545-63) enjoined due payment of tithes, and excommunicated those who withheld them.

It is interesting and significant that the principal cause that led Martin Luther, on October 31, 1517, to nail his ninety-five theses to the door of the Castle Church in Wittenberg, Germany, was his opposition to the sale of indulgences. Pope Julius (1503-13) began the construction of the magnificent Church of St. Peter in Rome in 1506, but the work stopped for lack of funds. Pope Leo X (1513-21) undertook to raise the necessary funds through the sale of indulgences. England, France, and Spain refused to be taxed in this manner, but Germany yielded to the papal demands. Indulgence salesmen were appointed to collect funds, and it became a popular saying:

"Sobald der Pfennig im kasten klingt, Die seel' aus dem fegfeuer springt." Or, "Soon as the

money in the chest rings, the troubled soul from purgatory springs."

From Luther's ninety-five theses sprang the Protestant Reformation. A movement originally purposed, not to start a new religious order, but to simply reform the original one. But, again, it is more than interesting to note that the whole of the Protestant Reformation began over the misuses of money by the existing ecclesiastical church.

Of course, the effect of Luther's ninety-five theses grew far beyond anything he had ever imagined or desired: a split with the existing Roman Catholic Church and papacy, and the beginning of a whole new religious movement that would ultimately result in over 400 different denominations each claiming to be the guardian of truth.

Unfortunately, much of the doctrine of this new Protestantism was simply borrowed and slightly modified from existing Roman Catholic doctrine or policy. Especially was this true in regards to the tithe. The priest was replaced with the pastor or minister or preacher, and tithes continued to be imposed on the laity, again much as the "royal tax" of the ancient pagans, as a means to support the clergy and to build their great church buildings. Many were monuments to the monumental ego of a man, and most to the neglect and exclusion of the poor and the needy – the real Biblical purpose of the tithe.

What are some of the conclusions that we can draw thus far in our study?

1. Tithing was strictly a Jewish practice.
2. Its basic purpose was as an act of *tzedakah*, to support the poor and those in need.
3. It was not practiced outside the land of Israel.
4. After the destruction of the Temple, the practice of

tithing ceases in Judaism, although acts of charity [*tzedakah*] continued as a replacement for the sacrifices of the Temple.

5. The Church of the 1st century never practiced tithing.
6. Nothing in the writings of the *Ante-Nicene Fathers* indicates that the Church practiced tithing (100 CE-325 CE).
7. The earliest known imposition of tithes upon the Church was from the late 8th century.
8. The forced imposition of the tithe upon the Church was the product of a corrupt clergy within the Roman Catholic Church.

TITHING IN THE CHURCH TODAY

So, what about believers today in this most important matter of giving? Are they to follow the strict Jewish practice of tithing? If so, it means giving not ten percent, but 20 to 30 percent. The Church has made a fundamental mistake in trying to impose a Jewish custom on believers, not understanding what the real purpose of tithing was, how it was done, nor to whom it was to go. Because there has been so much erroneous information presented on the subject, believers have been largely ignorant as to what they are supposed to give, how they are supposed to give, and to whom they are to give – and worse, what it really means to prosper.

Many believers have been led to believe that in order to prosper one must be a good "giver" or a good tither. In some circles, unfortunately, believers have been brow-beaten over this subject, being instructed that if they really want to be spiritual – if they really want to prosper – the first criterion is to be a faithful tither. Additionally, they must give the first tenth of their income "into the storehouse" – which means the church they attend. Any additional funds that may be given over and above the tithe (these are called offerings) are to be directed through the "storehouse" and distributed in such a manner that the local congregation receives the credit.

To whom do we give, and how much? The first fact we need to clearly reestablish is that the "storehouse" is not necessarily to be equated with the local church. The second fact is that for those in the "kingdom," namely, those in fellowship with and ruled by Jesus Christ, their responsibility transcends that of the tithe under the *Old Testament* period. The tithe was a part of a Jewish practice that ended in Judaism after the destruction of the Temple, and to which the believer was never bound. It has significance for the Church of today only insofar as a certain principle was established in the laws of *terumah* and *ma'aser*. The principle was that of caring – ministering to the needs of all those who are a part of the family of God – and even beyond, to all who are in need.

Believers today should not be responsible for just the ten or the 20 percent according to *Old Testament* custom, but responsible for 100 percent. As the steward over those possessions which God has entrusted into his stewardship, the "good steward" in the Kingdom of God is responsible to be faithful in discharging the 100 percent.

How does one apply this in their daily life? Those who are spiritually oriented will minister first of all to the local congregation of which they are a part, and then, under the direction of the Spirit of God be led to all those outside the four walls of the Church into a world filled with those who are in need.

CHAPTER 3

PROSPERITY

In dealing with the subject of prosperity, there are three basic English words that demand our attention: prosper, prosperity, and prosperous. Each word is used in English to translate several Hebrew words. In order to correctly understand the biblical meaning of prosperity, we need to look at each Hebrew word and see how it is used in the *Bible*:

1. *Halach. Halach* is the Hebrew root meaning "to walk" or "to go." It literally means "to go on" or "to go forward." *Halach* is used in *Judges* 4:24 "And the hand of the children of Israel prospered [*halach*], and prevailed against Jabin the king of Canaan, until they had destroyed Jabin king of Canaan."

2. *Kasher. Kasher* comes from the same Hebrew root as kosher, which is used in relation to certain kinds of foods that are right and acceptable for consumption. *Kasher* also means that which is right, acceptable, or holy, as opposed to that which is unacceptable or

unholy. *Kasher* is found in *Ecclesiastes* 11:6: "In the morning sow your seed, and in the evening withhold not your hand, for you know not which shall prosper [*kasher*], either this or that, or whether they both shall be good." Here, *kasher* literally means "to be right" or "to be correct."

3. *Sakal.* *Sakal* is translated eight times in the *Old Testament* as "prosper." It literally means "to think or act wisely" or "to cause to act wisely." "Keep, therefore, the words of this covenant, to do them, that you may prosper [*sakal*] in all that you do" (*Deuteronomy* 29:9).

4. *Shalav.* *Shalav* is translated three times in the *Old Testament* as "prosper": *Psalms* 122:6; *Job* 12:6; and *Lamentations* 1:5. The passage in *Psalm* 122:6 is the most frequently quoted of the three. "Pray for the peace of Jerusalem: they shall prosper [*shalav*] that love thee." Another form of the verb *shalav* is found in *Psalm* 73:12. In *Psalm* 30:6, it appears as *shelev*, and in *Zechariah* 7:7 as *shalev*, all translated in these passages as prosper or prosperity. However, the word means "to be at rest," "to be at ease," "to be safe," "to be secure," or "security."

5. *Shalvah.* *Shalvah* is a word that is closely related to *shalav*, *shelev*, and *shalev*, all mentioned above. *Shalvah* is translated three times in the English as prosperity or prosper: *Psalm* 122:7; *Proverbs* 1:32; *Jeremiah* 22:21. "Peace be within your walls, and prosperity within your palaces" (*Psalm* 122:7). The meaning of *shalvah* is essentially the same as *shalav*: rest, ease, or security.

6. *Shalom.* Almost everyone has heard of the Hebrew word *shalom*, and knows that it means "peace." Few know of the vast range of meanings associated with the root *shalam*. *Shalom* is used in *2 Samuel* 11:7; *Job* 15:21; *Psalm* 35:27; *Psalm* 73:3; *Jeremiah* 33:9;

Zechariah 8:12. One of the favored passages used in reference to prosperity, and often quoted is: "Let the Lord be magnified, which hath pleasure in the prosperity [*shalom*] of His servant" (*Psalm* 35:27). Another form of the root is found in *Job* 8:6: "If you were pure and upright, surely now he would awake for you, and make the habitation of your righteousness prosperous (*shalom*)." The Lord says He rejoices in the fact that His people have *shalom*. But, what is the meaning of *shalom*? It means "complete," "whole," "full," and "perfect."

7. *Tov.* The word *tov* is translated into English as prosperity six times. It is found in *Deuteronomy* 23:6; *1 Kings* 10:7; *Job* 36:11; *Ecclesiastes* 7:14; *Lamentations* 3:17; and *Zechariah* 1:17. Typical of all the passages is the one in *Job* 36:11: "If they obey and serve Him, they shall spend their days in prosperity [*tov*], and their years in pleasures." In Hebrew, the word *tov* simply means "good." The days of all those that obey and serve Him shall be "good."

8. *Tsaleach. Tsaleach*, and its related form, *tselach*, is by far the most widely used word in the *Old Testament* that is translated in English as prosper, or prosperously. It is used, in its varying forms, approximately 55 times. In *Isaiah* 53:10, we read: "Yet it pleased the Lord to bruise him. He has put him to grief. When you shall make his soul an offering for sin, he shall see his seed, he shall prolong his days, and the pleasure of the Lord shall prosper (*tsaleach*) in his hand." In *Isaiah* 54:17, we read: "No weapon that is formed against you shall prosper [*tsaleach*], and every tongue that shall rise against you in judgment you shall condemn."

In the *Old Testament*, *tsaleach* appears in two different *binyanim*, or verbal constructions. As used in the above quoted Scriptures, it simply means "to prosper." In the following Scriptures it appears in the *hiphil* or causative construction of the verb. The *hiphil*, or causative construction means "to cause to prosper," as in the following: "And he said to me, The Lord, before whom I walk, will send His angel with you, and prosper [*tsaleach*] your way. And you shall take a wife for my son from my kindred, and from my father's house....And he said to them, do not hinder me, seeing the Lord has prospered [*tsaleach*] my way" (*Genesis* 24: 40,56).

In this context, what does it mean to be prosperous, or to be caused to be prosperous? Simply stated, *tsaleach* means "successful." This word is frequently used today in modern Hebrew as in the sentence, "*Ani lo hitslacti lehitkasher elav*," or, "I wasn't successful in reaching him [on the telephone]." In other words, the line was busy. I wasn't successful. *Derek tslecha* means, "May you have a successful journey," or, "bon voyage."

Tselach, mentioned above, is used in such passages as the following: "Be it known to the King that we went to the province of Judah, to the House of the Great God. It is being built with huge stones, with timber laid in the walls. This work goes on with diligence and prospers (*tselach*) in their hands" (*Ezra* 5:8). "And the elders of the Jews built, and prospered (*tselach*) through the prophesying of Haggai the prophet and Zechariah the son of Iddo. And they finished their building as commanded by the God of Israel, and the decree of Cyrus, and Darius, and Artaxerses, Kings of Persia" (*Ezra* 6:14). "So this Daniel prospered (*tselach*) in the reign of Darius, and in the reign of Cyrus the Persian" (*Daniel* 6:28). In the latter passage we note an individual, Daniel, prospering. Again, the meaning here is simply "successful."

As we move from Hebrew and the *Old Testament* into the Greek of the *New Testament*, we are surprised to note that this word, "prosper," is used in English only two times

– in *1 Corinthians* 16:2 and in *3 John* 2, "Let every one of you lay by him in store, as God has prospered him" (*1 Corinthians* 16:2). "Beloved, I wish above all things that you may prosper and be in health, even as your soul prospers" (*3 John* 2). In both passages the word translated "prosper" is the Greek word *euodomai*, the meaning of which is closely akin to that of the Hebrew word *halach*. *Eoudomai* comes from the Greek word *odos*, which means "a road" or "a way." *Euodomai* means literally, "May you have a good journey, or be advancing in the proper direction."

It is of the utmost importance for us in our study to now note that after we study all these words that are translated into English as "prosper," not one necessarily has anything to do with accumulating material possessions. Prosperity! We all desire it. But, the exciting fact is that once we understand what prosperity really is we can have it. How do we become prosperous? Is there any relation between giving and prosperity?

The Rabbis always believed that there were blessings accompanying tithing unto the Lord. And this belief is certainly expressed over and over again by Jesus, who was Himself a Rabbi: For example:

> Give, and it shall be given unto you; good measure, pressed down, and shaken together, and running over shall men give into your bosom. For with the same measure that ye mete withal it shall be measured to you again (*Luke* 6:38).

I believe that it is a fundamental biblical principle that as one gives, so does he prosper. In other words, when one faithfully discharges his responsibilities in the matter of stewardship, there are certain principles of prosperity that naturally follow. But, we must keep in mind what true prosperity is.

In order to prosper biblically, we have to come to grips with one very important fact: Abraham Lincoln was wrong. All men are not created equal! All men do not even have equal opportunities. We are all unique, each with our own special talents and abilities. If we wish to be prosperous, we must first realize this and further, understand who and what we are. "What is God's will for me, and where do I fit in His Kingdom?" You see, we are all marvelously and uniquely made, so that we are different from anyone else. Therefore, God's will for one person may not be the same as His will for somebody else.

There are all kinds of people in this world. There are one-talented people, five-talented people, and if we use this biblical understanding, this will assist in answering the question as to why not all God's children prosper alike. One person is wildly successful and accumulates great wealth. It seems everything he touches turns to gold. While over there another child of God is not even making ends meet. He is out of work, dependent on state welfare, and just getting by. Does this mean that one is more deserving, more spiritual than the other? No, and it doesn't even necessarily mean that one is prospering and the other is not, once we understand what true prosperity is. It may simply mean that one individual has talents in certain areas that enable him to accumulate greater material possessions than others. Or, it may be a circumstance of birth. He may have inherited great wealth. But, again, wealth and possessions are not to be equated with biblical prosperity.

To begin to prosper biblically, we must understand who we are. We are all God's children, created in His image and likeness. Our body is the temple of the Holy Spirit. The Apostle Paul writes: "Know ye not that your body is the temple of the Holy Spirit which is in you, which ye have of God" (*1 Corinthians* 6:19). Again he writes: "Christ in you, the hope of glory" (*Colossians* 1:27). Jesus Himself stated, in a passage pregnant with meaning: "Behold, the kingdom of God is within you" (*Luke* 17:21).

Notice who we are: the temple of the Holy Spirit, the Kingdom of God. It does not matter whether we are a one-talented, five-talented, or ten-talented person. We are important to God and to one another. But what of those who are not prosperous – those who give and yet do not receive?

We must, in order to prosper, get things in their proper perspective. It is the motive, the attitude behind our giving that determines our prosperity. Remember from the beginning of our study? We clearly stated and emphasized that the motive behind much giving today is wrong. Why? Because it is giving with a desire to get something in return. Our spirituality and prosperity are not going to be determined by the amount we give, but by the motive, the attitude in which it is given. A person might give a million dollars with the wrong motive and it will not be nearly as beneficial for him as the person who gives only one dollar with the right motive. Our basic motive or attitude in giving is the first fundamental key to prosperity.

Second, many people are not prospering because they are not following the Word of God, but rather the preachings of man on the subject. People are being told, "If you want to receive from God, if you want to prosper, if you want to have enough money to pay your bills on the first of the month, then you need to send in your 'seed faith offering' so we can receive it by the tenth of the month." Again, this type of teaching engenders the idea that if we don't give, we are not going to get, but if we do, we will. It's all wrong! Terribly wrong! And that is exactly why many are not prospering. They are making foolish decisions and acting on impulse, rather than knowing what the Word of God and common sense would have one do in the matter. People are running all over the country today, praying for this, and claiming that, and expecting God to do this, and believing for that

– and, in most instances, wondering why things are not happening, why they are not receiving, why they are not prospering. The simple answer is that the motive is wrong and they are not acting in accordance with God's Word or common sense on the matter.

Again, our prosperity has to do with our understanding of ourselves and our commission in the Kingdom of God. You see, we were never called to accumulate possessions or to be concerned with things, but to be concerned with people. Remember Jesus' words in *Matthew* 10: 7,8: "And as you go, preach; saying, the Kingdom of God is at hand. Heal the sick, cleanse the lepers, raise the dead, cast out demons. Freely you have received, freely give."

If you want to prosper, here is your key! You don't give in order to get. You give because you have been blessed, and you want to be a blessing in return! It is a fundamental principle: "Give, and it shall be given unto you; good measure, pressed down, and shaken together, and running over, shall men give into your bosom" (*Luke* 6:38).

You see, it's as simple as that. It does not make any difference whether you are a one-talented man or a ten-talented man – real prosperity begins in the Word of God, and then reaches outward in acts of *tzedakah* to all those in need. The mission of the Church is outward – out there. The church was never called to be a Bless Me Club or a Praise The Lord Society, but a dynamic organism – powerful, alive, and prosperous. And, that power and prosperity is within the reach of every child of God, once they know what real prosperity is.

What is real biblical prosperity? It means to advance, to go forward. It means to be *kosher*, to be acceptable, to be right, to be pure. It means to act wisely, to make the right decisions. It means to be successful – and we can all be successful, regardless of what our chosen profession might be. You can be a successful shoemaker, bus driver, grocery clerk, sales person, auto mechanic, secretary, business person, homemaker, or whatever – if God is at the heart and center of your life and lives within you. Prosperity means to be safe, to be secure, to be at ease or rest; it means to have peace – to have *shalom* – to be whole, to be complete – a wholeness and completeness through God who lives and dwells within. That is real prosperity, and, thank God, every child of God can have it. And, more importantly, once one understands what real prosperity is, it becomes of much more value than the mere accumulation of material possessions. Real prosperity is Life! Life with God and in God.

BIBLIOGRAPHY

Blackman, Phillip, *The Mishnah*, Judaica Press, New York, 2000.

Brown, Francis; Driver, S. R.; Briggs, Charles A., *Brown-Driver-Briggs Hebrew and English Lexicon*, Hendrickson Publishers, Massachusetts, 1996.

Encyclopedia Britannica, Encyclopedia Britannica Inc., 2003.

Hallam, Henry, *View of the State of Europe During the Middle Ages*, Harper and Brothers, New York, 1854.

Kelsey, Morton T., *Healing And Christianity - In Ancient Thought And Modern Times*, Harper & Row, New York, 1976.

Qualben, Lars P., *A History of the Christian Church*, Wipf & Stock Publishers, Eugene, Oregon, 2008.

Roberts, Alexander and Donaldson, James (editors), *The Ante-Nicene Fathers*, Hendrickson Publishers, Massachusetts, 1994.

Roundell, Earl of Selborne, *Ancient Facts and Fictions Concerning Churches and Tithes*, MacMillan and Co., London and New York, 1892.

Schaff, Philip, *History of the Christian Church*, Hendrickson Publishers, Massachusetts, 2006.

Selden, John, *The Historie of Tithes,* London, 1618, Facsimile edition, Theatrum Orbis Terrarum Ltd. New York, Amsterdam and Da Capo Press, 1969.

Singer, Isidore (editor), *The Jewish Encyclopedia*, Funk and Wagnalls, New York, 1906.

Whiston, William (translator), *Josephus: Complete Works - Illustrated*, Kregel Publications, Grand Rapids, Michigan, 1976.

World Book Encyclopedia, World Book, Inc., 2010.

Young, Robert, *Young's Analytical Concordance to the Bible*, Hendrickson Publishers, Massachusetts, 1984.

ABOUT THE AUTHOR

 Dr. Roy B. Blizzard is President of Bible Scholars, Inc., an Austin-based corporation dedicated to biblical research and education. A native of Joplin, Missouri, he attended Oklahoma Military Academy and has a B.A. degree from Phillips University in Enid, Oklahoma. He has an M.A. degree from Eastern New Mexico University in Portales, New Mexico, an M.A. degree from the University of Texas at Austin, and a Ph.D. in Hebrew Studies from the University of Texas at Austin. From 1968 to June 1974, he was an instructor in Hebrew, Biblical History and Biblical Archaeology at the University of Texas at Austin. Dr. Blizzard is today a professor at the American Institute for Advanced Biblical Studies in Little Rock, Arkansas.

Dr. Blizzard has spent much of his time in Israel and the Middle East in study and research. He has hosted over 500 television programs about Israel and Judaism for various television networks and is a frequent television and radio guest. He is the author of numerous books and articles which can be found listed on the Bible Scholars Website, in the bookstore.

Dr. Blizzard is nationally certified as an educator in Marriage and Family relationships and human sexuality. He is a Diplomate with the American Board of Sexology and continues to conduct a private practice in the field of sex education and therapy.

OTHER BOOKS BY ROY B. BLIZZARD

The Bible Sex and You

Mishnah and the Words of Jesus

The Mountain of the Lord

Let Judah Go Up First: A Study in Praise, Prayer, and Worship

David Bivin and Roy Blizzard, Jr., *Understanding the Difficult Words of Jesus: New Insights From a Hebrew Perspective*

Bible Scholars, Inc.
P. O. Box 204073
Austin, Texas 78720

www.biblescholars.org

Dedicated to supporting, developing and promoting future Bible Scholars.